L2
Mathematics

Multiplication

D1708802

This book belongs to

_____

For information regarding permission, write to:
Scholastic Education International (Singapore) Pte Ltd
81 Ubi Avenue 4, #02-28 UB.ONE, Singapore 408830
Email: education@scholastic.com.sg

For sales enquiries write to:
Latin America, Caribbean, Europe (except UK), Middle East and Africa
Scholastic International
557 Broadway, New York, NY 10012, USA
Email: intlschool@scholastic.com

Rest of the World
Scholastic Education International (Singapore) Pte Ltd
81 Ubi Avenue 4 #02-28 UB.ONE Singapore 408830
Email: education@scholastic.com.sg

First edition 2013
Reprinted 2014

ISBN 978-981-07-1366-9

Welcome to Learning Express!

Helping your child build essential skills is easy!

These teacher-approved activities have been specially developed to make learning both accessible and enjoyable. On each page, you'll find:

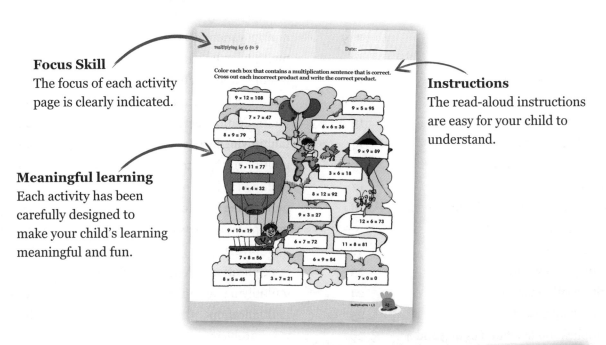

Focus Skill
The focus of each activity page is clearly indicated.

Meaningful learning
Each activity has been carefully designed to make your child's learning meaningful and fun.

Instructions
The read-aloud instructions are easy for your child to understand.

This book also contains:

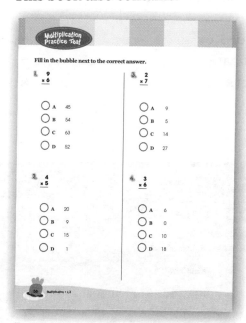

Instant assessment to ensure your child really masters the skills.

Completion certificate to celebrate your child's leap in learning.

Motivational stickers to mark the milestones of your child's learning path.

Contents

Multiplication

Multiplying is a quick way to add things up. For example:
2 + 2 + 2 + 2 + 2 = 10 or 2 × 5 = 10. The activities in this book
will introduce your child to some basic multiplication facts.

What to do

Have your child solve the vertical and horizontal multiplication
problems on the activity pages. Some of the problems will
require that your child carry over a number from one column
to the column on the left.

On the activity pages your child is asked to color each page
according to the answers to the problems. Doing so will
uncover a beautiful design.

Keep On Going!

Encourage your child to climb the multiplication mountain.
Have him or her practice the multiplication table from 1 to 10.
Then you and your child can make up problems for each other
to solve.

Date: _____

The addition sentence 4 + 4 + 4 + 4 + 4 = 20 can be written as a multiplication sentence. Count how many times 4 is being added together. The answer is 5. So, 4 + 4 + 4 + 4 + 4 = 20 can be written as 5 × 4 = 20. Multiplication is a quick way to add.

Write a multiplication sentence for each addition sentence.

1. **5 + 5 + 5 = 15**

2. **6 + 6 + 6 + 6 = 24**

3. **8 + 8 = 16**

4. **2 + 2 + 2 + 2 = 8**

5. **7 + 7 + 7 = 21**

6. **4 + 4 + 4 + 4 = 16**

7. **9 + 9 + 9 = 27**

8. **5 + 5 + 5 + 5 + 5 = 25**

9. **3 + 3 + 3 + 3 + 3 = 15**

10. **10 + 10 + 10 + 10 = 40**

11. **1 + 1 + 1 + 1 + 1 = 5**

12. **11 + 11 + 11 = 33**

13. **8 + 8 + 8 + 8 = 32**

14. **0 + 0 + 0 + 0 = 0**

15. **12 + 12 + 12 + 12 = 48**

16. **9 + 9 + 9 + 9 = 36**

 Today, we are going to the beach. Mom packed the picnic basket with six sandwiches, six water bottles, six candy bars and six apples. How many items did she pack in all?

Date: _____

 The multiplication symbol (×) can be thought of as meaning "groups of."

3 "groups of" 4 equals 12.
3 × 4 = 12

5 "groups of" 2 equals 10.
5 × 2 = 10

Write the multiplication sentence for each diagram.

1.

_____

2.

_____

3.

_____

4.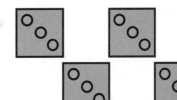

_____

5.

_____

6.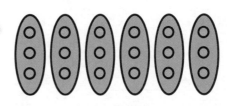

_____

Date: _____

Write the multiplication sentence for each diagram.

1.

_____

2.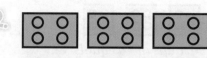

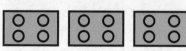

_____

3.

_____

4.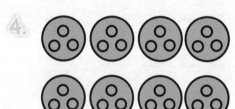

_____

5.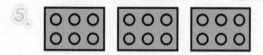

_____

6.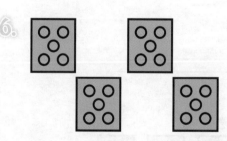

_____

Date: _____

Write the multiplication sentence for each diagram.

1.

2.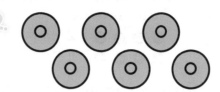

_____ _____

3.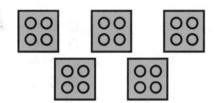

4.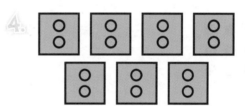

_____ _____

5.

6.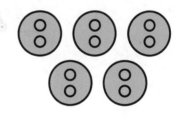

_____ _____

William has five bags of hamburgers. There are seven hamburgers in each bag. On another sheet of paper, draw pictures to show the total number of hamburgers.

Date: _____

 *An **array** demonstrates a multiplication sentence. The first **factor** tells how many rows there are. The second **factor** tells how many there are in each row. The answer of a multiplication sentence is called the **product**.*

$2 \times 4 = 8$ ○ ○ ○ ○ *2 rows*
           ○ ○ ○ ○ *4 in each row*

Write the multiplication sentence for each array.

1.
○ ○ ○
○ ○ ○

_____

2.
○ ○ ○
○ ○ ○
○ ○ ○

_____

3.
○ ○
○ ○
○ ○
○ ○

_____

4.
○ ○ ○ ○ ○ ○
○ ○ ○ ○ ○ ○
○ ○ ○ ○ ○ ○

_____

5.
○ ○ ○

_____

6.
○ ○ ○
○ ○ ○
○ ○ ○
○ ○ ○

_____

7.
○ ○ ○ ○ ○ ○
○ ○ ○ ○ ○ ○

_____

8.
○ ○ ○ ○
○ ○ ○ ○
○ ○ ○ ○

_____

9.
○ ○ ○ ○ ○ ○
○ ○ ○ ○ ○ ○
○ ○ ○ ○ ○ ○

_____

10.
○ ○ ○
○ ○ ○
○ ○ ○
○ ○ ○

_____

11.
○
○
○
○
○

_____

12.
○ ○
○ ○
○ ○
○ ○
○ ○
○ ○

_____

It was time for our family photo. The photographer arranged us into four rows. There were six people in each row. How many people in all were in the photo? On another piece of paper, draw an array to solve this problem.

Date: _____

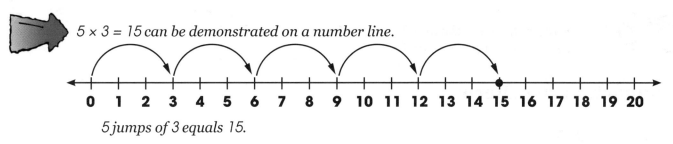

5 × 3 = 15 can be demonstrated on a number line.

5 jumps of 3 equals 15.

Write the multiplication sentence demonstrated on each number line.

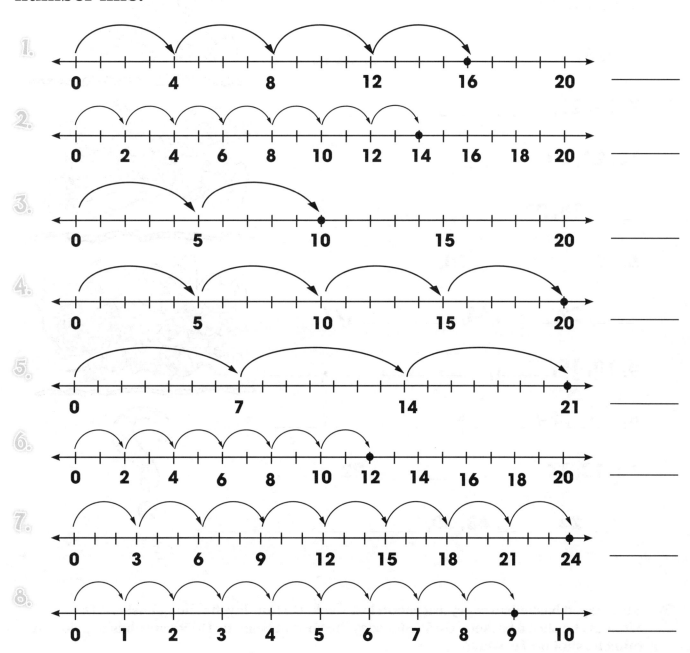

Date: _____

What is the pattern for the numbers 0, 2, 4, 6, 8, 10, 12, 14, 16, 18?
The pattern shows multiples of 2.

Complete each pattern.

1. **3, 6, 9, 12,** _____, _____, _____, _____, _____

2. **4, 8, 12, 16,** _____, _____, _____, _____, _____

3. **1, 2, 3, 4,** _____, _____, _____, _____, _____

4. **7, 14, 21,** _____, _____, _____, _____, _____

5. **10, 20, 30,** _____, _____, _____, _____, _____

6. _____, **18, 27,** _____, _____, _____, _____

7. **6, 12,** _____, _____, **30,** _____, _____, _____

8. _____, **22,** _____, **44,** _____, _____, **77**

9. **5, 10, 15,** _____, _____, _____, _____, _____

10. **8,** _____, **24,** _____, **40,** _____, _____, _____

11. **10, 12, 14,** _____, _____, _____, **22,** _____, _____

12. _____, **24,** _____, **48, 60,** _____, _____, _____, _____

Sam played basketball every afternoon last week. On Sunday, he shot 3 baskets. On Monday, he shot 6 baskets. On Wednesday, he shot 12 baskets. How many baskets do you think he shot on Tuesday?

Date: _____

When a number is multiplied by 0, the product is always 0. When a number is multiplied by 1, the product is always the number being multiplied.

Multiply. Shade all products of 0 yellow. Shade all other products green.

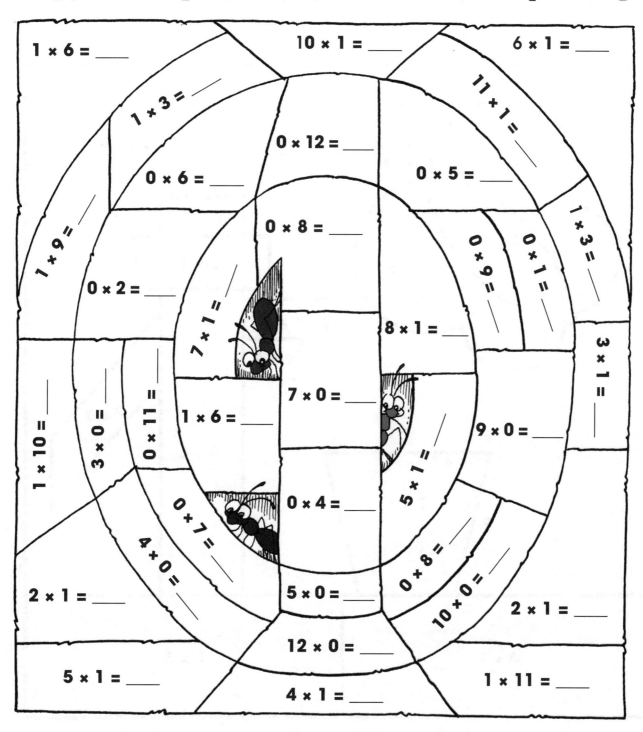

1 × 6 = ___

10 × 1 = ___

6 × 1 = ___

1 × 3 = ___

11 × 1 = ___

0 × 12 = ___

0 × 6 = ___

0 × 5 = ___

1 × 9 = ___

0 × 8 = ___

1 × 3 = ___

0 × 2 = ___

0 × 9 = ___

0 × 1 = ___

7 × 1 = ___

8 × 1 = ___

3 × 1 = ___

1 × 10 = ___

3 × 0 = ___

0 × 11 = ___

1 × 6 = ___

7 × 0 = ___

9 × 0 = ___

5 × 1 = ___

0 × 7 = ___

0 × 4 = ___

4 × 0 = ___

0 × 8 = ___

2 × 1 = ___

5 × 0 = ___

10 × 0 = ___

2 × 1 = ___

12 × 0 = ___

5 × 1 = ___

4 × 1 = ___

1 × 11 = ___

Date: _____

Find the products. Then use your answer and the code below to color the diagram.

0, 2 = red   1, 3, 5 = orange   4, 6 = green

7, 8 = yellow   9 = black   10 = blue

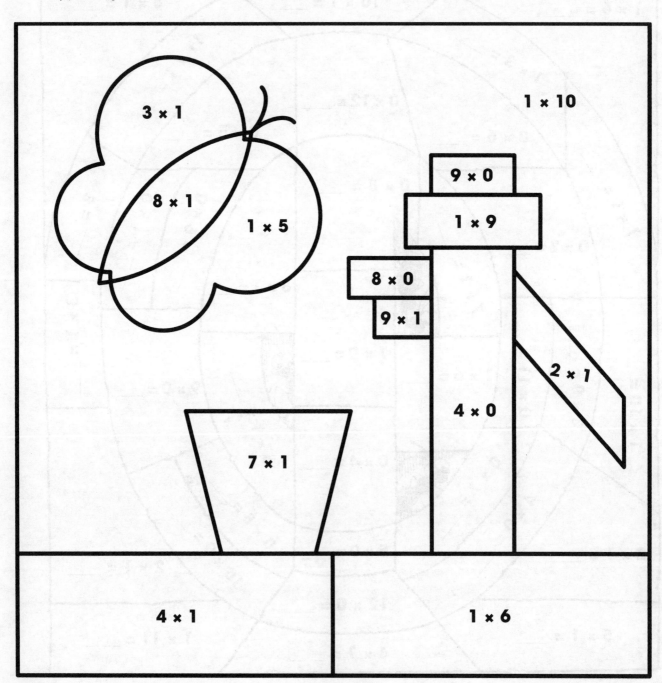

Date: _____

When multiplying by 2, skip count by 2 or think of number line jumping!

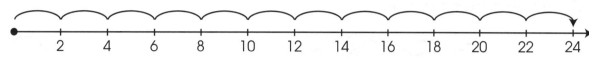

Multiply.

1. 2 × 3 = ____   2 × 8 = ____   11 × 2 = ____   2 × 7 = ____

2. 8 × 2 = ____   4 × 2 = ____   2 × 2 = ____   2 × 4 = ____

3. 12 × 2 = ____   5 × 2 = ____   10 × 2 = ____   2 × 12 = ____

4. 9 × 2 = ____   2 × 1 = ____   2 × 10 = ____   7 × 2 = ____

5. 2 × 0 = ____   2 × 6 = ____   3 × 2 = ____   0 × 2 = ____

6. 2 × 5 = ____   2 × 9 = ____

7. 6 × 2 = ____   1 × 2 = ____

8. 2 × 11 = ____   2 × 2 = ____

 On another piece of paper, write a rhyme to go with each multiplication fact of 2. Examples: "2 × 4 = 8, I love math. Can you relate?" Or, "2 × 4 = 8, I've got to go, and shut the gate!"

Date: _____

Color each cloud with a correct multiplication sentence to show the path to the space station.

2 × 3 = 6

12 × 2 = 24

1 × 2 = 1

6 × 2 = 8

2 × 9 = 11

8 × 2 = 16

4 × 2 = 8

2 × 7 = 14

11 × 2 = 22

2 × 5 = 10

2 × 6 = 12

3 × 2 = 5

2 × 8 = 14

7 × 2 = 12

2 × 10 = 20

2 × 2 = 4

2 × 12 = 26

9 × 2 = 18

2 × 1 = 2

Eight pilots each flew a plane across the Atlantic Ocean. Each pilot invited one passenger to fly with her. How many people in all flew across the Atlantic Ocean?

Date: _____

Find the products. Then use the code below to color the diagram.

6, 8, 10, 12 = red   14, 16 = purple

18, 20 = yellow   22, 24 = green

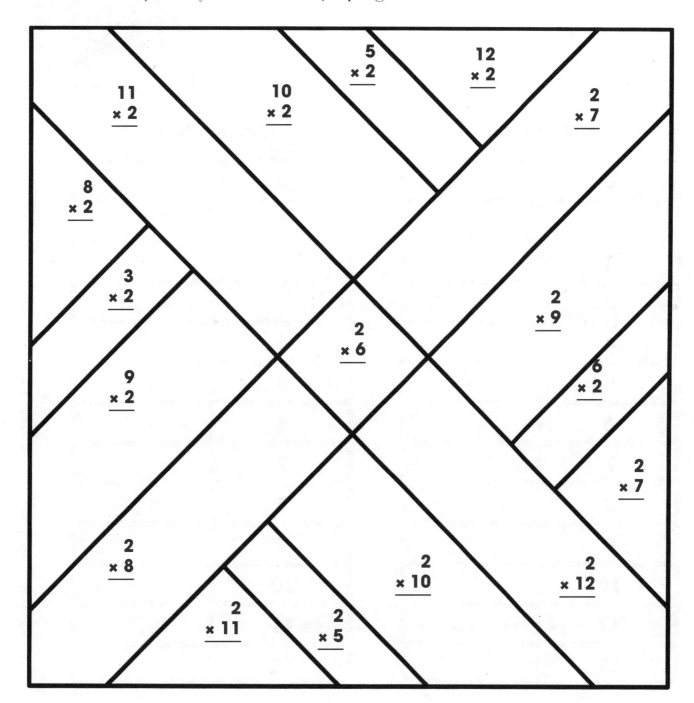

Multiply each number in the column by the number at the top.
Write your answers in the column on the right.

Multiply!

Multiply by 1

0	
1	
2	
3	
4	
5	
6	
7	
8	
9	
10	
11	
12	

Multiply by 2

0	
1	
2	
3	
4	
5	
6	
7	
8	
9	
10	
11	
12	

Date: _____

Solve the multiplication problems. Then match each product with a letter in the key below. Write the correct letters on the blanks below to answer the riddle.

30	11	36	18	32	8	15	0	27	6	42	24	33	6	12
O	A	H	I	F	K	O	I	O	S	N	T	O	Q	W

1. **5 × 3** = ☐

2. **2 × 3** = ☐

3. **8 × 3** = ☐

4. **4 × 3** = ☐

5. **9 × 3** = ☐   6. **6 × 3** = ☐

7. **10 × 3** = ☐   8. **12 × 3** = ☐

9. **11 × 3** = ☐   10. **0 × 3** = ☐

What did the owl say when someone knocked on its door?

" ___ ___ ___ ___ ___ ___   ___ ___   ___ ___ ?"
  4   8   5   9   1   7   10   2   6   3

Date: _____

Multiply.

START →

3 × 12 = _____

3 × 4 = _____

3 × 9 = _____

3 × 0 = _____

9 × 3 = _____

6 × 3 = _____

2 × 3 = _____

8 × 3 = _____

4 × 3 = _____

5 × 3 = _____

3 × 3 = _____

3 × 1 = _____

3 × 10 = _____

3 × 6 = _____

12 × 3 = _____

3 × 8 = _____

1 × 3 = _____

7 × 3 = _____

3 × 5 = _____

10 × 3 = _____

3 × 11 = _____

0 × 3 = _____

3 × 4 = _____

6 × 3 = _____

8 × 3 = _____

3 × 12 = _____

3 × 3 = _____

3 × 7 = _____

3 × 2 = _____

10 × 3 = _____

3 × 9 = _____

11 × 3 = _____

 The Three Factory paints one stack of boxes every three minutes. How many minutes does it take the factory to paint nine stacks of boxes?

Date: _____

What should you say if you are asked, "Do you want to learn the 3s?"
To find out, look at each problem below. If the product is correct, color
the space green. If the product is incorrect, color the space yellow.

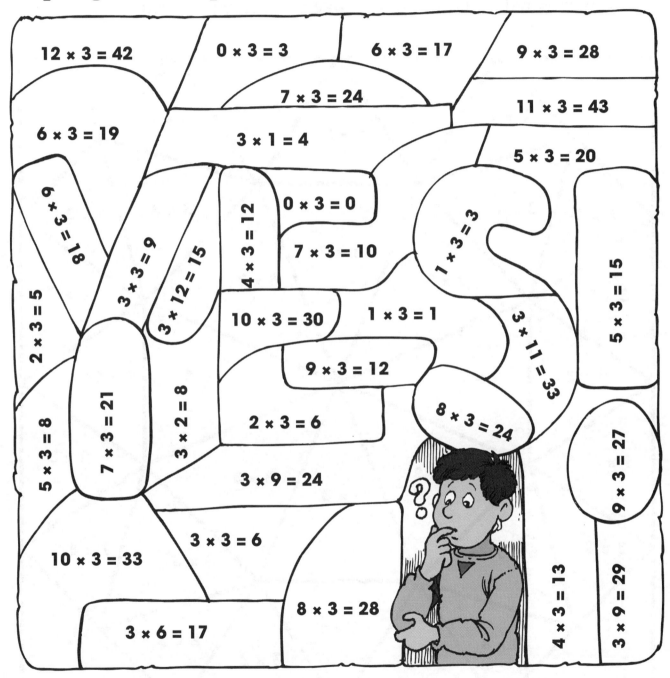

 How many letters are in the answer to the puzzle? If you wrote this word ten times, how many letters would you write altogether?

Date: _____

Multiply. Use the code to color the shapes. After you color this design, you'll see the shape of the morning star.

3, 6, 27 = red   12, 15, 18 = orange   9, 21, 24 = green

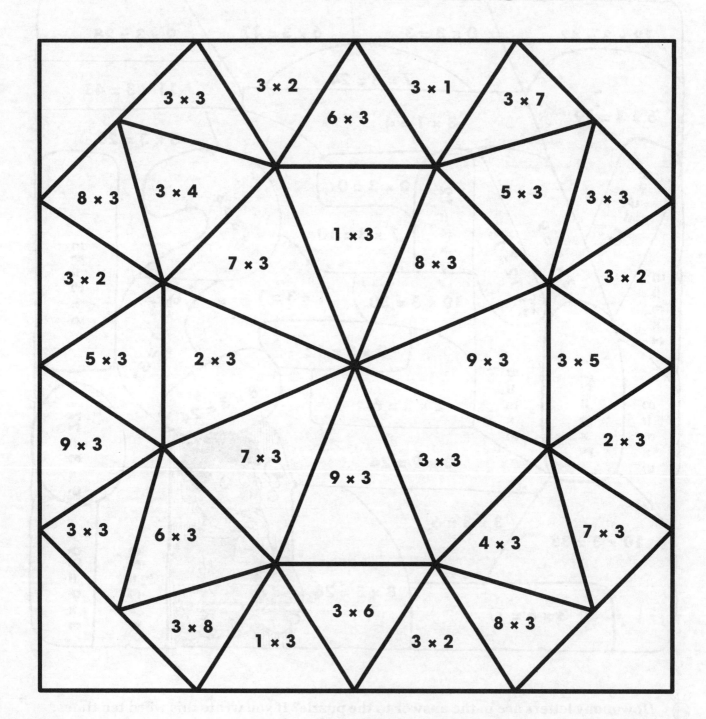

Date: _____

Multiply.

1. $\begin{array}{r} 2 \\ \times\ 7 \\ \hline \end{array}$

2. $\begin{array}{r} 10 \\ \times\ 3 \\ \hline \end{array}$

3. $\begin{array}{r} 9 \\ \times\ 1 \\ \hline \end{array}$

Multiply!

4. $\begin{array}{r} 2 \\ \times\ 3 \\ \hline \end{array}$

5. $\begin{array}{r} 8 \\ \times\ 3 \\ \hline \end{array}$

6. $\begin{array}{r} 1 \\ \times\ 6 \\ \hline \end{array}$

7. $\begin{array}{r} 12 \\ \times\ 2 \\ \hline \end{array}$

8. $\begin{array}{r} 4 \\ \times\ 3 \\ \hline \end{array}$

9. $\begin{array}{r} 4 \\ \times\ 0 \\ \hline \end{array}$

10. $\begin{array}{r} 7 \\ \times\ 3 \\ \hline \end{array}$

11. $\begin{array}{r} 3 \\ \times\ 9 \\ \hline \end{array}$

12. $\begin{array}{r} 2 \\ \times\ 5 \\ \hline \end{array}$

Date: _____

To answer this question, multiply. Then use the code to write the letter of each multiplication sentence on the blank above its product.

A 4 × 10 =	I 4 × 0 =	O 4 × 7 =	T 4 × 8 =
D 4 × 4 =	M 4 × 2 =	R 4 × 6 =	Y 4 × 9 =
E 4 × 11 =	N 4 × 5 =	S 4 × 3 =	! 4 × 12 =

___ ___ ___ ___   ___   ___ ___ ___ ___ ___   ___ ___
36   44   12   48   0   40   16   28   24   44   0   32

___ ___ ___ ___   ___ ___ ___   ___ ___ ___ ___ ___
 8   28   24   44   40   20   16   8   28   24   44   48

💡 On another piece of paper, write a message to a friend. Make a code using the multiplication facts of 4. Have your friend use the code to read the message.

Date: _____

Find the products. Then use your answer and the color code below to color the design.

0, 4, 8 = brown

24, 28, 32, 36, 40, 44 = blue

12, 16, 20 = red

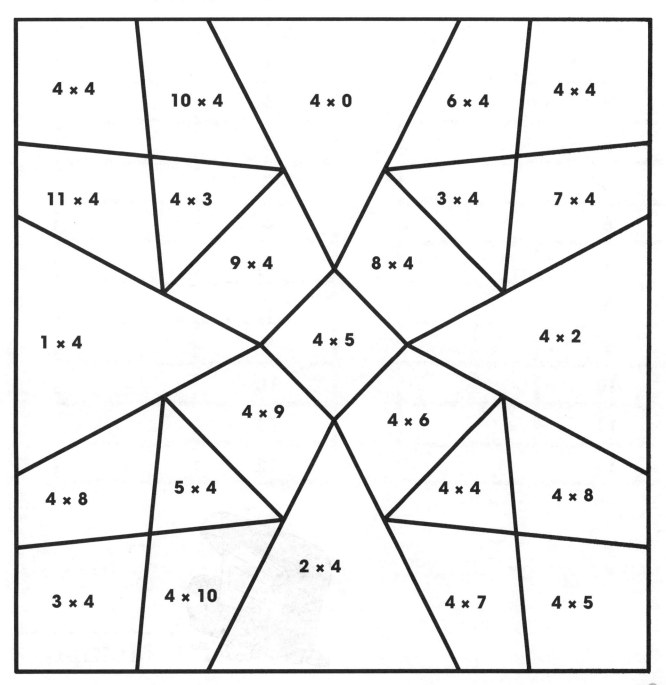

Date: _____

Multiply each number in the column by the number at the top. Write your answers in the column on the right.

Multiply by 3	
0	
1	
2	
3	
4	
5	
6	
7	
8	
9	
10	
11	
12	

Multiply by 4	
0	
1	
2	
3	
4	
5	
6	
7	
8	
9	
10	
11	
12	

Multiply!

Date: _____

Multiply.

Multiply!

1.   8
    × 4

2.   10
    × 2

3.   9
    × 3

4.   6
    × 4

5.   9
    × 2

6.   5
    × 3

7.   4
    × 9

8.   4
    × 7

9.   10
    × 4

10.   4
    × 0

11.   5
    × 1

12.   3
    × 7

Date: _____

Look at the number chart below. Starting with 1, count 5 squares. Color in the fifth square. Then count 5 more squares and color in the fifth square. Keep going until you reach 100.

1	2	3	4	5	6	7	8	9	10
11	12	13	14	15	16	17	18	19	20
21	22	23	24	25	26	27	28	29	30
31	32	33	34	35	36	37	38	39	40
41	42	43	44	45	46	47	48	49	50
51	52	53	54	55	56	57	58	59	60
61	62	63	64	65	66	67	68	69	70
71	72	73	74	75	76	77	78	79	80
81	82	83	84	85	86	87	88	89	90
91	92	93	94	95	96	97	98	99	100

Tally marks can be arranged in groups of five, like this: ⫿⫿⫿ ⫿⫿⫿ ⫿⫿⫿ 
Then you can count by fives.

1. Count how many girls and boys are in your class. Draw tally marks in groups of five.
   Girls: _____   Boys: _____

2. Now count the total number. Write the totals here:
   Girls: [ ]   Boys: [ ]

Date: _____

To find out what letter stands for 'math' and 'multiplication', complete each problem. Join the dots in order from least to greatest.

5 × 2 =
___

5 × 4 =
___

5 × 1 = •
___

5 × 5 =
___

5 × 11 =
___

5 × 8 =
___

5 × 3 =
___

5 × 10 =
___

5 × 9 =
___

5 × 0 = •━━━━━•
___

5 × 12 =
___

5 × 7 =
___

5 × 6 =
___

 There are five children in line to buy an ice-cream cone. If each child buys a cone with three scoops of ice cream, how many total scoops of ice cream will the store sell?

Date: _____

Multiply. Then trace a path to Finish by finding all the products less than 30.

Start

$5 \times 0 =$

$5 \times 3 =$

$7 \times 5 =$

$5 \times 2 =$

$5 \times 0 =$

$6 \times 5 =$

$5 \times 1 =$

$5 \times 10 =$

$5 \times 5 =$

$5 \times 6 =$

$5 \times 7 =$

$5 \times 4 =$

$5 \times 12 =$

$11 \times 5 =$

Finish

$2 \times 5 =$

multiplying by 5

Date: _____

Find the products. Color the shapes using the code.

0 to 20 = yellow   25 to 40 = green   45 to 60 = orange

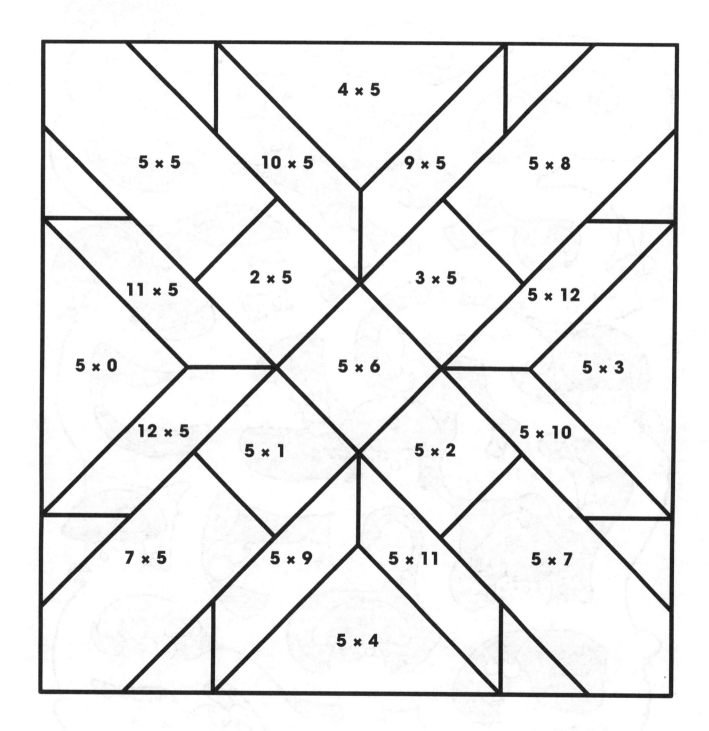

Date: _____

Multiply. Then follow the path from each multiplication sentence to its product.

4 × 5 = ____

8 × 5 = ____

4 × 1 = ____

3 × 7 = ____

6 × 5 = ____

2 × 0 = ____

5 × 11 = ____

3 × 9 = ____

3 × 8 = ____

2 × 4 = ____

Date: _____

*Let's review some more! The numbers being multiplied are called **factors**. The answer is called the **product**.*

Multiply. Use the code to write the letter of each multiplication sentence on the blank above its product and answer the riddle.

A 3 × 12 =	H 2 × 9 =	O 3 × 7 =	U 2 × 12 =
B 5 × 10 =	I 4 × 7 =	P 1 × 0 =	W 5 × 5 =
D 2 × 8 =	L 5 × 6 =	R 2 × 11 =	Y 4 × 12 =
E 4 × 11 =	M 4 × 8 =	S 5 × 7 =	! 3 × 3 =
G 2 × 6 =	N 3 × 9 =	T 5 × 9 =	

Why did the math teacher choose multiplication to help his class grow?

‾35‾ ‾21‾   ‾45‾ ‾18‾ ‾36‾ ‾45‾   ‾18‾ ‾28‾ ‾35‾   ‾12‾ ‾22‾ ‾21‾ ‾24‾ ‾0‾

‾25‾ ‾21‾ ‾24‾ ‾30‾ ‾16‾   ‾50‾ ‾44‾ ‾12‾ ‾28‾ ‾27‾   ‾45‾ ‾21‾

‾12‾ ‾44‾ ‾45‾   ‾30‾ ‾36‾ ‾22‾ ‾12‾ ‾44‾ ‾22‾   ‾36‾ ‾27‾ ‾16‾

‾32‾ ‾24‾ ‾30‾ ‾45‾ ‾28‾ ‾0‾ ‾30‾ ‾48‾ ‾9‾

On the field trip to the Science Museum, Mr Weaver divided his class into six groups. Mrs Moore divided her class into five groups. Each group had four students. How many students are in each class? Which class has more students? Solve the problem on another piece of paper.

Date: _____

Multiply. Then use the code to write the letter of each multiplication sentence on the blank above its product and answer the riddle.

A	2 × 11 =	H	5 × 12 =	S	5 × 9 =
B	1 × 7 =	I	2 × 6 =	T	5 × 7 =
C	2 × 9 =	M	4 × 11 =	U	4 × 7 =
D	4 × 12 =	O	3 × 7 =	V	3 × 11 =
E	4 × 9 =	P	5 × 8 =	Y	3 × 8 =
G	4 × 4 =	R	5 × 6 =	!	5 × 0 =

Why is multiplication quality math?

__ __ __ __ __ __ __   __ __ __   __ __ __ __
7 36 18 22 28 45 36   24 21 28   60 22 33 36

__ __ __   __ __ __ __ __   __ __ __ __ __ __ __
35 60 36   30 12 16 60 35   40 30 21 48 28 18 35

__ __ __ __ __   __ __ __ __ __
36 33 36 30 24   35 12 44 36 0

 Andrew bought nine packages of crackers. There were four crackers in each package. How many crackers did he buy altogether?

Date: _____

Multiply. On another piece of paper, find the sum of the products of each star trail. Then use the code to color each star to match its star trail sum.

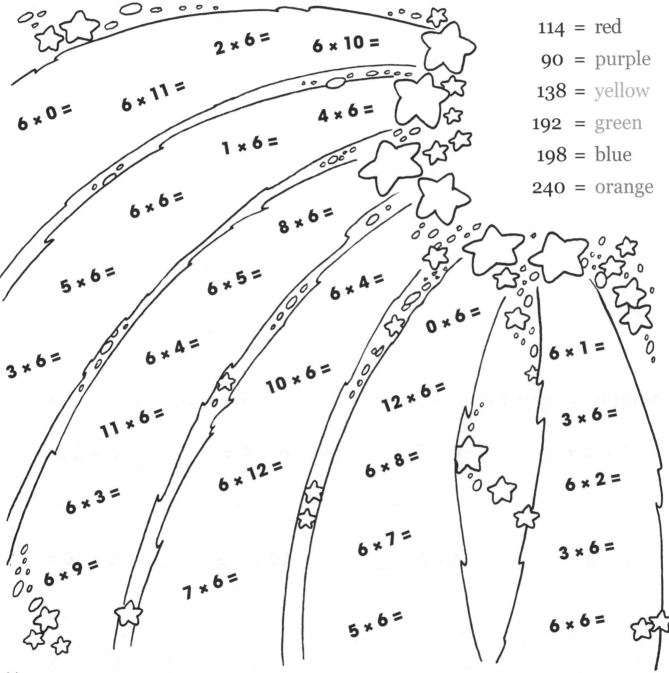

2 × 6 =

6 × 10 =

6 × 0 =

6 × 11 =

4 × 6 =

1 × 6 =

6 × 6 =

8 × 6 =

5 × 6 =

6 × 5 =

6 × 4 =

3 × 6 =

6 × 4 =

0 × 6 =

6 × 1 =

11 × 6 =

10 × 6 =

12 × 6 =

3 × 6 =

6 × 3 =

6 × 12 =

6 × 8 =

6 × 2 =

6 × 7 =

3 × 6 =

6 × 9 =

7 × 6 =

5 × 6 =

6 × 6 =

114 = red

90 = purple

138 = yellow

192 = green

198 = blue

240 = orange

Emma counted the fireworks she watched at the fireworks show. She counted 6 different fireworks every 15 minutes. The firework show lasted 2 hours. How many fireworks did Emma see?

Date: _____

Using the code below, write a multiplication sentence for each message.

≋	●	⊠	☺	⇐	★	✓	⅄	↙	◗	☺	Υ	⌘
0	1	2	3	4	5	6	7	8	9	10	11	12

1. ☺ × ✓ = ● ↙
_____

2. ✓ × ★ = ☺ ≋
_____

3. ◗ × ✓ = ★ ⇐
_____

4. Υ × ✓ = ✓ ✓
_____

5. ✓ × ⊠ = ● ⊠
_____

6. ⇐ × ✓ = ⊠ ⇐
_____

7. ↙ × ✓ = ⇐ ↙
_____

8. ⅄ × ✓ = ⇐ ⊠
_____

9. ✓ × ⌘ = ⅄ ⊠
_____

10. ≋ × ✓ = ≋
_____

11. ● × ✓ = ✓
_____

12. ☺ × ✓ = ✓ ≋
_____

Multiply. Then use the code above to write each multiplication sentence.

13. $5 \times 6 =$ _____

14. $6 \times 7 =$ _____

15. $6 \times 9 =$ _____

16. $6 \times 3 =$ _____

_____ _____ _____ _____

17. $6 \times 8 =$ _____

18. $6 \times 6 =$ _____

19. $12 \times 6 =$ _____

20. $6 \times 10 =$ _____

_____ _____ _____ _____

Abby wrote the same message to 6 different friends. She made a code using flower symbols for each of the 12 letters in her message. How many total flower symbols did she write?

Date: _____

Multiply each number in the column by the number at the top. Write your answers in the column on the right.

Multiply by 5	
0	
1	
2	
3	
4	
5	
6	
7	
8	
9	
10	
11	
12	

Multiply by 6	
0	
1	
2	
3	
4	
5	
6	
7	
8	
9	
10	
11	
12	

Multiply!

Date: _____

Multiply.

1. 10
   × 6

2. 5
   × 3

3. 7
   × 2

Multiply!

4. 5
   × 2

5. 8
   × 3

6. 2
   × 6

7. 9
   × 5

8. 10
   × 4

9. 3
   × 3

10. 2
    × 0

11. 3
    × 9

12. 5
    × 5

Date: _____

Multiply.

1. 2
    × 4
    ___

2. 3
    × 6
    ___

3. 10
    × 5
    ___

Multiply!

4. 7
    × 6
    ___

5. 4
    × 7
    ___

6. 0
    × 6
    ___

7. 4
    × 8
    ___

8. 3
    × 2
    ___

9. 4
    × 4
    ___

10. 3
    × 5
    ___

11. 5
    × 8
    ___

12. 4
    × 6
    ___

Date: _____

Multiply.

7 × 2 = _____

1 × 7 = _____

8 × 7 = _____

12 × 7 = _____

7 × 5 = _____

7 × 9 = _____

7 × 10 = _____

0 × 7 = _____

7 × 11 = _____

7 × 12 = _____

7 × 7 = _____

7 × 8 = _____

3 × 7 = _____

9 × 7 = _____

7 × 4 = _____

11 × 7 = _____

6 × 7 = _____

 Maurice was asked to build seven statues in front of City Hall. Each statue would take him six months to finish. He needs to complete the statues before the Music Festival which will be held in exactly two years. How many months will Maurice need to complete the statues? Will he have enough time?

Date: _____

Multiply.

7 × 9 = ____

11 × 7 = ____

6 × 7 = ____

7 × 4 = ____

3 × 7 = ____

7 × 7 = ____

7 × 10 = ____

7 × 0 = ____

5 × 7 = ____

7 × 12 = ____

7 × 2 = ____

4 × 7 = ____

7 × 11 = ____

1 × 7 = ____

0 × 7 = ____

7 × 8 = ____

2 × 7 = ____

7 × 1 = ____

7 × 6 = ____

8 × 7 = ____

9 × 7 = ____

10 × 7 = ____

12 × 7 = ____

7 × 3 = ____

7 × 5 = ____

Cassandra's space mission is to orbit Earth seven times, as quickly as she can, a total of seven times. How many times altogether will she orbit Earth?

Date: _____

Multiply.

0 to 10 = purple   21 to 30 = blue   41 to 50 = yellow
61 to 70 = pink   11 to 20 = orange   31 to 40 = red
51 to 60 = green

4
× 6

5 × 2 = _____

2
× 6

3
× 7

7
× 3

7
× 1

6 × 8 = _____

3
× 6

5
× 6

6
× 5

4
× 7

7 × 5 = _____

3
× 7

6 × 6 = _____

9
× 7

6
× 7

6
× 4

3
× 7

7
× 9

7
× 7

9 × 6 = _____

8
× 6

7
× 6

8 × 7 = _____

5 × 6 = _____

7 × 4 = _____

Date: _____

Use a stopwatch to time how long it takes to multiply around the track.

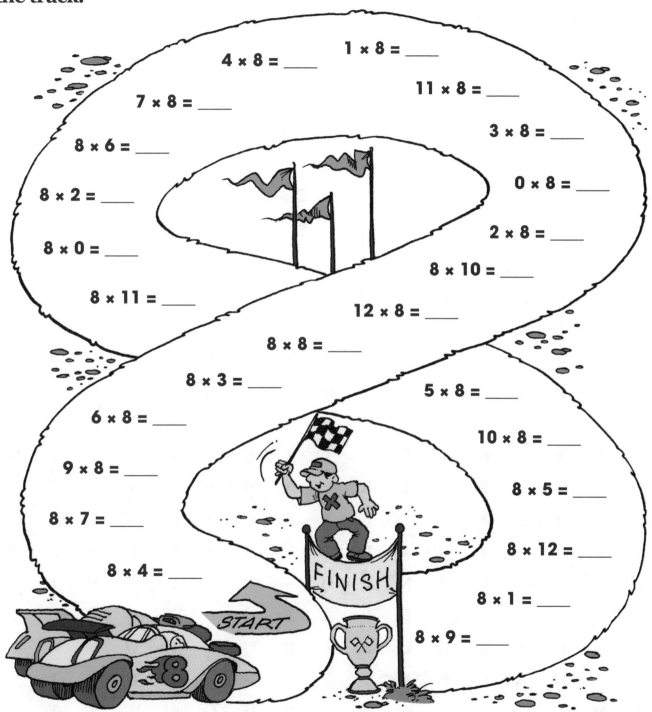

$4 \times 8 =$ ___

$1 \times 8 =$ ___

$11 \times 8 =$ ___

$7 \times 8 =$ ___

$3 \times 8 =$ ___

$8 \times 6 =$ ___

$0 \times 8 =$ ___

$8 \times 2 =$ ___

$8 \times 0 =$ ___

$2 \times 8 =$ ___

$8 \times 10 =$ ___

$8 \times 11 =$ ___

$12 \times 8 =$ ___

$8 \times 8 =$ ___

$8 \times 3 =$ ___

$5 \times 8 =$ ___

$6 \times 8 =$ ___

$10 \times 8 =$ ___

$9 \times 8 =$ ___

$8 \times 5 =$ ___

$8 \times 7 =$ ___

$8 \times 12 =$ ___

$8 \times 4 =$ ___

$8 \times 1 =$ ___

$8 \times 9 =$ ___

 Racing Ricardo rapidly raced 8 times around the Eight Track. It took him 12 seconds to rapidly race one time around the track. How many seconds did it take him to complete the race?

Date: _____

Multiply. Then circle the number word for each product in the puzzle. The words will go forward, backward, up, down and diagonally. Be careful; some products appear more than once!

1. 8 × 2 = _____   4 × 8 = _____   8 × 4 = _____   10 × 8 = _____

2. 0 × 8 = _____   5 × 8 = _____   8 × 6 = _____   9 × 8 = _____

3. 8 × 1 = _____   8 × 3 = _____   2 × 8 = _____   11 × 8 = _____

4. 1 × 8 = _____   8 × 12 = _____   3 × 8 = _____   6 × 8 = _____

5. 8 × 5 = _____   8 × 8 = _____   8 × 0 = _____

6. 8 × 9 = _____   8 × 7 = _____   8 × 8 = _____

```
F C E L I M R U O F – Y T N E W T
O O F O R T Y – E I G H T I F E H
R N I S I X C B I F N E E T X I S
T S F I J W E I G H T S T S O G I
Y I T X T F H R H S Z E R O W H L
– O Y T W V O S T I U V W V T T R
E W – E E U I R Y X B E X Y – Y U
I T S E N S M L T T C N A Z Y – O
G – I N T H I R T Y – T W O T E F
H Y X X Y Z N P Q – D Y J N N I –
T T Y Y – T E R A F E – F Q E G Y
H R D T F D U R Z O G T K O V H T
G I H R O F V Y O U F W L U E T X
I H Y O U E W X C R H O M W S T I
E T L F R N I N E T Y – S I X Z S
```

Date: _____

Multiply the each number in the column by the number at the top.
Write your answers in the column on the right.

Multiply!

Multiply by 7

0	
1	
2	
3	
4	
5	
6	
7	
8	
9	
10	
11	
12	

Multiply by 8

0	
1	
2	
3	
4	
5	
6	
7	
8	
9	
10	
11	
12	

Date: _____

Is there a pattern of the products when multiplying by 9? Yes! The sum of each product equals 9! There are two exceptions. One exception is 11 × 9 = 99; then each number in the product is 9! What is the other exception?

0 × 9 =   0
1 × 9 =   9
2 × 9 = |1| 8
3 × 9 = |2| 7
4 × 9 = |3| 6
5 × 9 = |4| 5
6 × 9 = |5| 4
7 × 9 = |6| 3
8 × 9 = |7| 2
9 × 9 = |8| 1
10 × 9 = |9| 0

THERE SEEMS TO BE A PATTERN HERE.

Unscramble the number word for each product of the following 9s multiplication facts. Then write the 9s fact next to the number word.

1. **ENO DDHNUER TEHGI** _____ _____

2. **NYTENI-NNEI** _____ _____

3. **TINENY** _____ _____

4. **YITHEG-NOE** _____ _____

5. **EENTVSY-WOT** _____ _____

6. **YXTIS-ERETH** _____ _____

7. **TFFIY-RUOF** _____ _____

8. **YTRFO-EVIF** _____ _____

9. **YHRTTI-XIS** _____ _____

On another piece of paper, write the pattern for the multiplication facts of the number words above. Then write the remaining 9s multiplication facts to complete the pattern.

Date: _____

Multiply. Write the number word for each product in the puzzle. Don't forget the hyphens!

Across

1. **9 × 5 =** _____   5. **1 × 9 =** _____
7. **9 × 12 =** _____   8. **9 × 10 =** _____
10. **2 × 9 =** _____   11. **9 × 11 =** _____

Down

2. **9 × 3 =** _____   3. **6 × 9 =** _____
4. **0 × 9 =** _____   6. **9 × 8 =** _____
9. **9 × 9 =** _____

Date: _____

Find the products. Then use your answer and the code below to color the diagram.

9, 18, 27 = blue   63, 72 = green
36, 45, 54 = yellow   81, 90, 99 = red

Date: _____

Multiply. Then use the code to write the letter of each multiplication sentence on the blank above its product and answer the riddle.

A	1 × 6 =	G	4 × 4 =	M	6 × 12 =	S	9 × 3 =
C	5 × 9 =	H	8 × 8 =	N	7 × 7 =	T	8 × 12 =
D	7 × 8 =	I	10 × 9 =	O	2 × 6 =	U	9 × 9 =
E	5 × 5 =	K	3 × 12 =	P	9 × 2 =	Y	9 × 12 =
F	4 × 6 =	L	7 × 12 =	R	12 × 5 =	!	0 × 3 =

What is the best way to learn multiplication?

___ ___ ___ ___   ___ ___ ___   ___ ___ ___ ___ ___
24 90 49 56   96 64 25   60 90 16 64 96

___ ___ ___ ___ ___ ___ ___ ___ ,   ___ ___ ___
18 60 12 56 81 45 96 27   16 25 96

___ ___ ___ ___   ___ ___   ___ ___ ___ ___ ___
96 64 25 72   96 12   27 96 90 45 36

___ ___   ___ ___ ___ ___   ___ ___ ___ ___ ,
90 49   108 12 81 60   64 25 6 56

___ ___ ___   ___ ___ ___ ___   ___ ___ ___
6 49 56   56 12 49 96   84 25 96

___ ___ ___ ___   ___ ___ ___ ___ ___ ___ ___
96 64 25 72   25 27 45 6 18 25 0

ACME
MULTIPLICATION
TUTOR

Date: _____

Multiply.

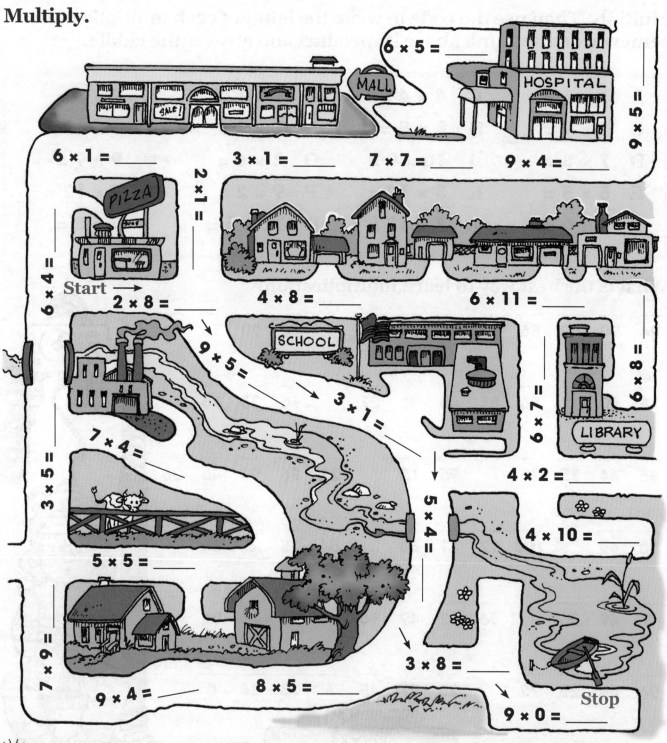

6 × 5 = _____

9 × 5 = _____

6 × 1 = _____   3 × 1 = _____   7 × 7 = _____   9 × 4 = _____

2 × 1 = _____

6 × 4 = _____

Start →

2 × 8 = _____   4 × 8 = _____   6 × 11 = _____

9 × 5 = _____

6 × 8 = _____

6 × 7 = _____

3 × 1 = _____

7 × 4 = _____

3 × 5 = _____

5 × 5 = _____

5 × 4 = _____

4 × 2 = _____

4 × 10 = _____

7 × 9 = _____

9 × 4 = _____   8 × 5 = _____   3 × 8 = _____

Stop

9 × 0 = _____

After finishing three slices of pizza at the restaurant, James walked to the pond to meet his dad. James and his dad were going to go canoeing. Add the products on the road James walked along from the pizza restaurant to the pond. Follow the arrows. What multiplication fact has a product equal to this sum?

Date: _____

Find out, what would be the most exciting way to get to Multiplication Island. Multiply. Then join the dots in order from 10 to 42.

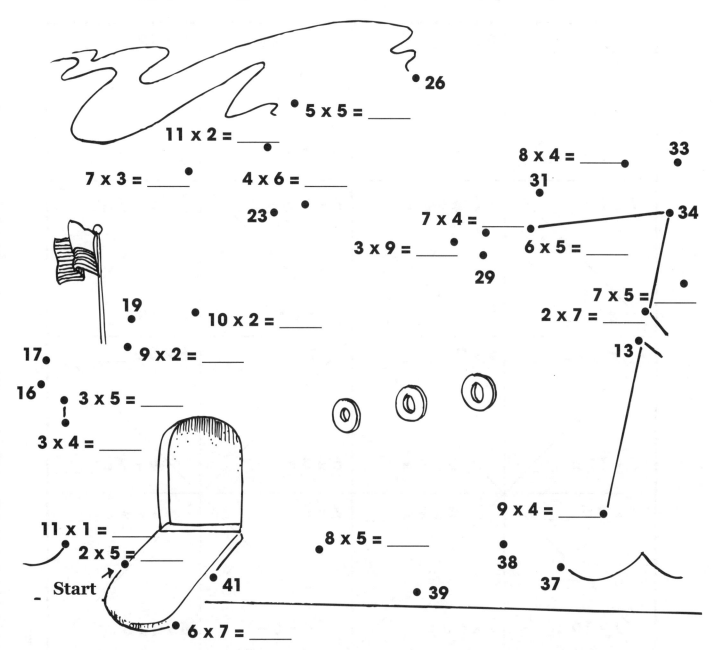

• 26

5 x 5 = _____

11 x 2 = _____

8 x 4 = _____ 33

7 x 3 = _____ 4 x 6 = _____ 31

23 7 x 4 = _____ 34

3 x 9 = _____ 6 x 5 = _____

29

19 7 x 5 = _____

10 x 2 = _____ 2 x 7 = _____

17 9 x 2 = _____ 13

16 3 x 5 = _____

3 x 4 = _____

11 x 1 = _____ 9 x 4 = _____

2 x 5 = _____ 8 x 5 = _____ 38

Start 41 37

_ 39

6 x 7 = _____

Max and his family traveled to Multiplication Island and stayed for three days. One day Max discovered seven banana plants and five coconut palm trees. He picked six bananas from each banana plant and four coconuts from each coconut palm tree. On another piece of paper, find out how many total bananas Max picked. How many total coconuts did he pick?

Date: _____

Multiply. Color each triangle with an even product orange. Color each triangle with an odd product blue.

8 × 6 = ___   9 × 4 = ___   8 × 9 = ___   8 × 12 = ___

7 × 9 = ___   7 × 7 = ___   9 × 3 = ___   9 × 11 = ___

7 × 7 = ___   4 × 6 = ___   8 × 7 = ___   1 × 7 = ___

8 × 8 = ___   9 × 5 = ___   5 × 7 = ___   8 × 10 = ___

6 × 9 = ___   9 × 9 = ___   7 × 3 = ___   6 × 6 = ___

7 × 11 = ___   5 × 8 = ___   6 × 3 = ___   9 × 7 = ___

1 × 9 = ___   5 × 9 = ___   7 × 5 = ___   3 × 9 = ___

7 × 10 = ___   7 × 6 = ___   9 × 8 = ___   6 × 12 = ___

 Maria was decorating a picture frame for her friend's birthday. She chose seven different-sized, diamond-shaped tiles to glue around the frame. There was enough room to glue four colors of each size of tile. How many tiles did she use altogether to decorate the frame? On another piece of paper, solve this problem and draw a picture of what the frame might look like.

Date: —————

**Color each box that contains a multiplication sentence that is correct.
Cross out each incorrect product and write the correct product.**

9 × 12 = 108

9 × 5 = 95

7 × 7 = 47

6 × 6 = 36

8 × 9 = 79

9 × 9 = 89

7 × 11 = 77

3 × 6 = 18

8 × 4 = 32

8 × 12 = 92

9 × 3 = 27

12 × 6 = 73

9 × 10 = 19

6 × 7 = 72

11 × 8 = 81

7 × 8 = 56

6 × 9 = 54

8 × 5 = 45

3 × 7 = 21

7 × 0 = 0

Date: _____

 Multiplying by 10 is really easy! Multiply the factor by 1 and add a 0.
$10 \times 8 =$ _____ (Multiply $1 \times 8 = 8$, and add a zero. The product is 80.)
$10 \times 12 =$ _____ (Multiply $1 \times 12 = 12$, and add a zero. The product is 120.)

Multiply. Then color each space with a product less than 50 red. Color each space with a product greater than 70 orange. Color each space with a product equal to 50 yellow.
Color all other spaces with a multiplication sentence green.

$10 \times 2 =$

$10 \times 0 =$

$10 \times 4 =$

$10 \times 1 =$

$10 \times 5 =$

$3 \times 10 =$

$10 \times 5 =$

$4 \times 10 =$

$5 \times 10 =$

$2 \times 10 =$

$10 \times 3 =$

$12 \times 10 =$

$8 \times 10 =$

$10 \times 12 =$

$1 \times 10 =$

$0 \times 10 =$

$8 \times 10 =$

$10 \times 8 =$

$5 \times 10 =$

$10 \times 10 =$

$10 \times 6 =$

$10 \times 11 =$

$9 \times 10 =$

$10 \times 6 =$

$6 \times 10 =$

$10 \times 9 =$

$11 \times 10 =$

$7 \times 10 =$

$7 \times 10 =$

$10 \times 10 =$

$10 \times 6 =$

$6 \times 10 =$

$10 \times 7 =$

multiplication facts of 10

When multiplying by 10, the product always ends in 0.

Multiply.

7 × 10 = _____

10 × 0 = _____

10 × 9 = _____

1 × 10 = _____

9 × 10 = _____

3 × 10 = _____

10 × 5 = _____

10 × 8 = _____

HANG TEN!

10 × 2 = _____

10 × 4 = _____

10 × 3 = _____

10 × 10 = _____

8 × 10 = _____

6 × 10 = _____

WAY COOL!

0 × 10 = _____

4 × 10 = _____

10 × 7 = _____

COOL!

11 × 10 = _____

10 × 1 = _____

10 × 12 = _____

10 × 10 = _____

10 × 11 = _____

2 × 10 = _____

12 × 10 = _____

5 × 10 = _____

10 × 6 = _____

Every morning Miranda chose her favorite ten clouds in the sky. She especially liked clouds which looked like animals. If Miranda did this every morning for a week, how many clouds did she choose altogether?

Date: _____

Find the products. Color using the code.

10 to 40 = brown   50 to 70 = green   80 to 100 = blue

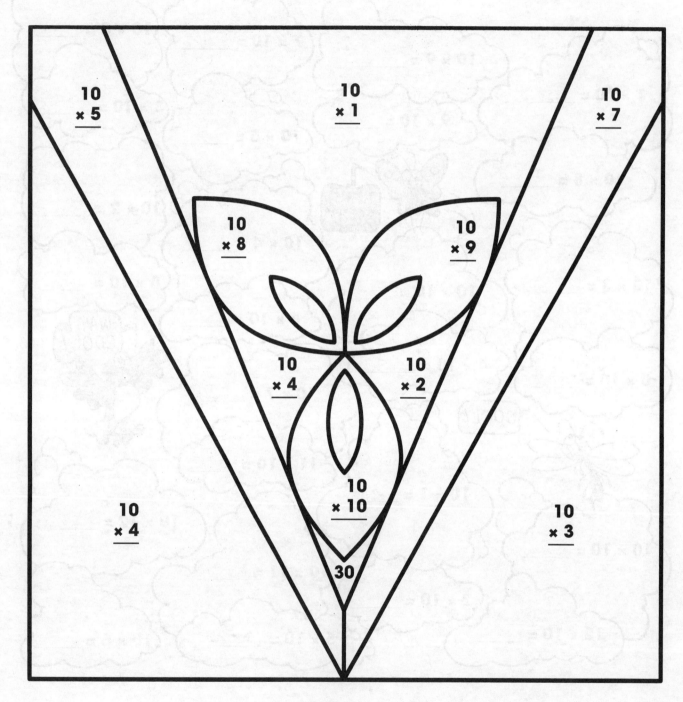

$$\begin{array}{c} 10 \\ \times\ 5 \\ \hline \end{array}$$

$$\begin{array}{c} 10 \\ \times\ 1 \\ \hline \end{array}$$

$$\begin{array}{c} 10 \\ \times\ 7 \\ \hline \end{array}$$

$$\begin{array}{c} 10 \\ \times\ 8 \\ \hline \end{array}$$

$$\begin{array}{c} 10 \\ \times\ 9 \\ \hline \end{array}$$

$$\begin{array}{c} 10 \\ \times\ 4 \\ \hline \end{array}$$

$$\begin{array}{c} 10 \\ \times\ 2 \\ \hline \end{array}$$

$$\begin{array}{c} 10 \\ \times\ 10 \\ \hline \end{array}$$

$$\begin{array}{c} 10 \\ \times\ 4 \\ \hline \end{array}$$

$$\begin{array}{c} 10 \\ \times\ 3 \\ \hline \end{array}$$

30

Date: _____

Multiply each number in the column by the number at the top.
Write your answers in the column on the right.

Multiply!

Multiply by 9	
0	
1	
2	
3	
4	
5	
6	
7	
8	
9	
10	
11	
12	

Multiply by 10	
0	
1	
2	
3	
4	
5	
6	
7	
8	
9	
10	
11	
12	

Date: _____

Multiply.

Multiply!

1. 2
   × 5

2. 6
   × 4

3. 8
   × 8

4. 10
   × 7

5. 9
   × 5

6. 7
   × 2

7. 9
   × 9

8. 6
   × 5

9. 3
   × 8

10. 0
    × 10

11. 4
    × 7

12. 3
    × 6

Date: _____

Multiply.

1.   4
      × 8

2.   10
     × 8

3.   10
     × 4

Multiply!

4.   3
      × 7

5.   0
      × 9

6.   2
      × 6

7.   5
      × 4

8.   7
      × 0

9.   7
      × 7

10.   3
      × 9

11.   9
      × 2

12.   5
      × 8

Multiplication

Date: _____

Multiply. Join the flowers with the same product.

multiplication

Date: _____

Multiply. Write the answer for each product in the puzzle.

Across

1. **3 × 7 =**
3. **6 × 2 =**
6. **8 × 8 =**
9. **9 × 9 =**
11. **9 × 5 =**
13. **6 × 7 =**
15. **7 × 9 =**
18. **11 × 5 =**
21. **12 × 2 =**
23. **10 × 4 =**

Down

2. **4 × 4 =**
4. **10 × 2 =**
5. **3 × 6 =**
7. **11 × 4 =**
10. **2 × 7 =**
12. **7 × 8 =**
14. **5 × 5 =**
16. **6 × 6 =**
17. **3 × 8 =**
19. **9 × 6 =**

Date: _____

Solve the multiplication problems. Then match each product with a letter in the key below. Write the correct letters on the blanks below to answer the riddle.

10	13	11	16	5	27	8	6	9	24	20	7	12	0	18
F	C	O	E	A	U	E	K	B	F	W	D	T	O	T

1. **5 × 1** = ☐

2. **8 × 1** = ☐

3. **11 × 1** = ☐

4. **0 × 1** = ☐

5. **3 × 2** = ☐   6. **5 × 2** = ☐

7. **6 × 2** = ☐   8. **8 × 2** = ☐

9. **9 × 2** = ☐   10. **12 × 2** = ☐

What did the rocket say when it left the party?

"TIM ___ ___ ___ ___ ___ ___ ___ ___ ___."
　　　8　7　3　9　1　5　2　4　6　10

Date: _____

Fill in the blanks.

1. How many legs on

   | 1 turkey | _____ | 3 turkeys | _____ |
   | 2 turkeys | _____ | 4 turkeys | _____ |

2. How many legs on

   | 1 cat | _____ | 3 cats | _____ |
   | 2 cats | _____ | 4 cats | _____ |

3. How many legs on

   | 1 ladybug | _____ | 3 ladybugs | _____ |
   | 2 ladybugs | _____ | 4 ladybugs | _____ |

4. How many legs on

   | 1 spider | _____ | 3 spiders | _____ |
   | 2 spiders | _____ | 4 spiders | _____ |

5. How many legs on

1 squid	_____	6 squid	_____
2 squid	_____	7 squid	_____
3 squid	_____	8 squid	_____
4 squid	_____	9 squid	_____
5 squid	_____	10 squid	_____

Date: _____

Jack's class was growing bean plants. After 1 week, Jack's was the tallest.

Measure Jack's plant below. Record its height: ☐

After 2 weeks, Jack's plant had doubled in height.

How tall was it now? ☐

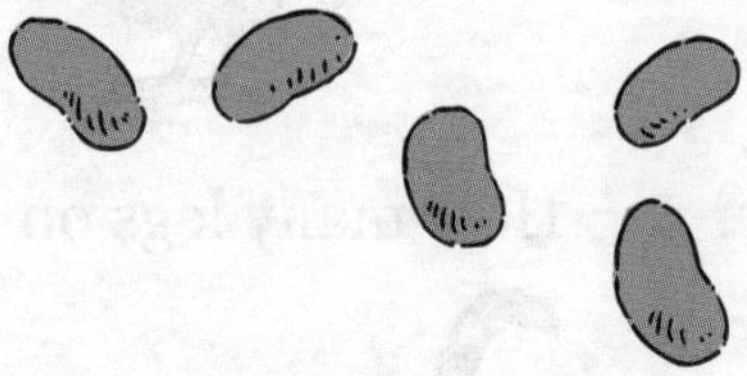

Draw a picture to show how tall the plant grew. Measure your drawing to make sure it is the correct height.

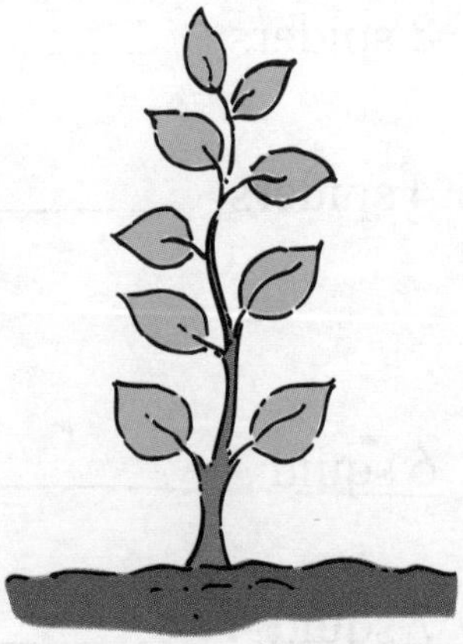

2 weeks

After 3 weeks, Jack's plant was still growing!

How tall would it be now? ☐

Explain your answer. _____

_____

Date: _____

Write a multiplication sentence for each question.

1. Josie's class is going to the teddy bear factory.
   Three children will ride in each car. There are 3 cars.

   How many children are going to the teddy bear factory? _____

2. Pete's class is going to see the elephant seals.
   Five children will ride in each van. There are 3 vans.

   How many children are going to see the elephant seals? _____

3. Rosa's class is going to the Space Museum.
   Eight children will ride in each small bus. There are 2 small buses.

   How many children are going to the Space Museum? _____

Read the questions. Write the multiplication sentence for each question and solve the problem.

1. Sally earns $5 a week walking her neighbor's dog.
   How much will she earn in a month?
   (Assume there are 4 weeks in a month.)

2. A scoop of ice cream cost $1.
   Toby bought one scoop for himself, one scoop for his brother and two scoops for his parents.
   How much did Toby spend altogether?

3. Trisha saves $2 more than her sister every week.
   How much more will she save than her sister after 10 weeks?

Date: _____

Read the questions. Write the multiplication sentence for each question and solve the problem.

1. A worker can pack 12 toys in one hour.
   How many toys can the worker pack between 9 a.m. and 12 noon?

2. Mother buys 5 dozen loaves of bread for a party.
   How many loaves of bread does Mother buy?

3. Jane, Christine and Myla have 8 DVDs each.
   How many DVDs do they have altogether?

Fill in the bubble next to the correct answer.

1.
$$\begin{array}{r} 9 \\ \times\,6 \\ \hline \end{array}$$

   ○ **A**   45

   ○ **B**   54

   ○ **C**   63

   ○ **D**   52

3.
$$\begin{array}{r} 2 \\ \times\,7 \\ \hline \end{array}$$

   ○ **A**   9

   ○ **B**   5

   ○ **C**   14

   ○ **D**   27

2.
$$\begin{array}{r} 4 \\ \times\,5 \\ \hline \end{array}$$

   ○ **A**   20

   ○ **B**   9

   ○ **C**   15

   ○ **D**   1

4.
$$\begin{array}{r} 3 \\ \times\,6 \\ \hline \end{array}$$

   ○ **A**   6

   ○ **B**   0

   ○ **C**   10

   ○ **D**   18

Fill in the bubble next to the correct answer.

 5. 6
         × 5

○ **A**   26

○ **B**   30

○ **C**   40

○ **D**   60

 7. 5
         × 10

○ **A**   50

○ **B**   15

○ **C**   5

○ **D**   20

6. 3
        × 7

○ **A**   17

○ **B**   21

○ **C**   10

○ **D**   11

8. 4
        × 4

○ **A**   4

○ **B**   8

○ **C**   12

○ **D**   16

Fill in the bubble next to the correct answer.

9. 12
    × 8

 ○ A   4

 ○ B   20

 ○ C   26

 ○ D   96

11. 10
    × 7

 ○ A   3

 ○ B   17

 ○ C   70

 ○ D   71

10. 7
    × 7

 ○ A   0

 ○ B   14

 ○ C   40

 ○ D   49

12. 4
    × 8

 ○ A   4

 ○ B   12

 ○ C   32

 ○ D   48

Fill in the bubble next to the correct answer.

13.
```
   9
 × 2
```

- ◯ **A** 7
- ◯ **B** 11
- ◯ **C** 18
- ◯ **D** 28

15.
```
   5
 × 3
```

- ◯ **A** 2
- ◯ **B** 8
- ◯ **C** 15
- ◯ **D** 50

14.
```
   7
 × 6
```

- ◯ **A** 13
- ◯ **B** 42
- ◯ **C** 67
- ◯ **D** 76

16.
```
  11
 × 4
```

- ◯ **A** 4
- ◯ **B** 14
- ◯ **C** 15
- ◯ **D** 44

 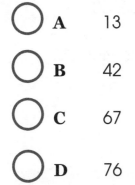

Multiplication Practice Test

Fill in the bubble next to the correct answer.

17. 12, 14, ____, ____, 20

- ◯ A   15, 16
- ◯ B   16, 18
- ◯ C   16, 19
- ◯ D   15, 19

19. 44, 55, 66, ____, ____

- ◯ A   77, 88
- ◯ B   88, 99
- ◯ C   67, 68
- ◯ D   77, 78

18. 25, ____, ____, 34, 37

- ◯ A   26, 27
- ◯ B   27, 29
- ◯ C   28, 31
- ◯ D   30, 32

20. 35, ____, 45, ____, 55

- ◯ A   40, 50
- ◯ B   40, 46
- ◯ C   36, 50
- ◯ D   36, 46

Write the multiplication sentence for each diagram.

21.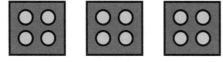

_____

22.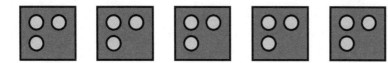

_____

23.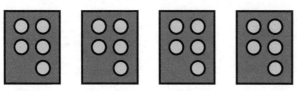

_____

Read the questions. Write the multiplication sentence for each question and solve the problem.

24. Jason walks 3 km every week.
How many km will she walk in 12 weeks?

25. A bookseller sold 10 storybooks.
Each storybook cost $7.
How much did he make?

26. Five children each bought 8 funfair tickets.
How many tickets did they buy in all?

Answer Key

Page 6

1. $3 \times 5 = 15$ 2. $4 \times 6 = 24$
3. $2 \times 8 = 16$ 4. $4 \times 2 = 8$
5. $3 \times 7 = 21$ 6. $4 \times 4 = 16$
7. $3 \times 9 = 27$ 8. $5 \times 5 = 25$
9. $5 \times 3 = 15$ 10. $4 \times 10 = 40$
11. $5 \times 1 = 5$ 12. $3 \times 11 = 33$
13. $4 \times 8 = 32$ 14. $4 \times 0 = 0$
15. $4 \times 12 = 48$ 16. $4 \times 9 = 36$;
$6 + 6 + 6 + 6 = 24$, $6 \times 4 = 24$

Page 7

1. $2 \times 4 = 8$ 2. $3 \times 3 = 9$
3. $3 \times 5 = 15$ 4. $4 \times 3 = 12$
5. $4 \times 1 = 4$ 6. $6 \times 3 = 18$

Page 8

1. $8 \times 2 = 16$ 2. $6 \times 4 = 24$
3. $2 \times 6 = 12$ 4. $8 \times 3 = 24$
5. $3 \times 6 = 18$ 6. $4 \times 5 = 20$

Page 9

1. $2 \times 2 = 4$ 2. $6 \times 1 = 6$
3. $5 \times 4 = 20$ 4. $7 \times 2 = 14$
5. $3 \times 5 = 15$ 6. $5 \times 2 = 10$

Page 10

1. $2 \times 3 = 6$ 2. $3 \times 3 = 9$
3. $4 \times 2 = 8$ 4. $3 \times 5 = 15$
5. $1 \times 3 = 3$ 6. $4 \times 3 = 12$
7. $2 \times 6 = 12$ 8. $3 \times 4 = 12$
9. $3 \times 6 = 18$ 10. $5 \times 3 = 15$
11. $5 \times 1 = 5$ 12. $7 \times 2 = 14$;
24 people, Check array

Page 11

1. $4 \times 4 = 16$ 2. $7 \times 2 = 14$
3. $2 \times 5 = 10$ 4. $4 \times 5 = 20$
5. $3 \times 7 = 21$ 6. $6 \times 2 = 12$
7. $8 \times 3 = 24$ 8. $9 \times 1 = 9$

Page 12

1. 15, 18, 21, 24, 27
2. 20, 24, 28, 32, 36
3. 5, 6, 7, 8, 9
4. 28, 35, 42, 49, 56

5. 40, 50, 60, 70, 80
6. 9, 36, 45, 54, 63
7. 18, 24, 36, 42, 48
8. 11, 33, 55, 66
9. 20, 25, 30, 35, 40
10. 16, 32, 48, 56, 64
11. 16, 18, 20, 24, 26
12. 12, 36, 72, 84, 96, 108; 9 goals

Page 13

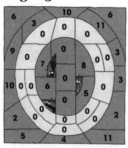

Page 14

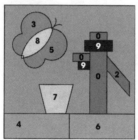

Page 15

1. 6, 16, 22, 14   2. 16, 8, 4, 8
3. 24, 10, 20, 24   4. 18, 2, 20, 14
5. 0, 12, 6, 0   6. 10, 18
7. 12, 2   8. 22, 4; Rhymes will vary.

Page 16

$8 \times 1 = 8$, 8 people

Page 17

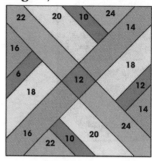

Page 18

Multiply by 1: 0, 1, 2, 3, 4, 5, 6, 7, 8, 9, 10, 11, 12;   Multiply by 2: 0, 2, 4, 6, 8, 10, 12, 14, 16, 18, 20, 22, 24

Page 19

1. 15   2. 6   3. 24   4. 12   5. 27
6. 18   7. 30   8. 36   9. 33   10. 0;
"WHOOOO IS IT?"

Page 20

$9 \times 3 = 27$

Page 21

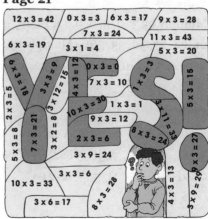

Page 22

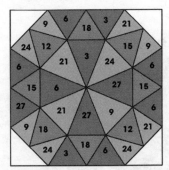

Page 23

1. 14   2. 30   3. 9   4. 6
5. 24   6. 6   7. 24   8. 12
9. 0   10. 21   11. 27   12. 10

Page 24

A. 40   D. 16   E. 44   I. 0
M. 8   N. 20   O. 28   R. 24
S. 12   T. 32   Y. 36   !. 48;
YES! I ADORE IT MORE AND
MORE!; Check message.

Page 25

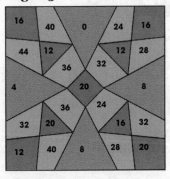

Page 26

Multiply by 3: 0, 3, 6, 9, 12, 15, 18,
21, 24, 27, 30, 33, 36;   Multiply by
4: 0, 4, 8, 12, 16, 20, 24, 28, 32, 36,
40, 44, 48

Page 27

1. 32   2. 20   3. 27   4. 24
5. 18   6. 15   7. 36   8. 28
9. 40   10. 0   11. 5   12. 21

Page 28

1	2	3	4	5	6	7	8	9	10
11	12	13	14	15	16	17	18	19	20
21	22	23	24	25	26	27	28	29	30
31	32	33	34	35	36	37	38	39	40
41	42	43	44	45	46	47	48	49	50
51	52	53	54	55	56	57	58	59	60
61	62	63	64	65	66	67	68	69	70
71	72	73	74	75	76	77	78	79	80
81	82	83	84	85	86	87	88	89	90
91	92	93	94	95	96	97	98	99	100

Answers will vary.

Page 29

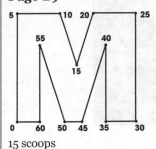

15 scoops

Page 30

Page 31

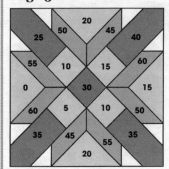

Page 32

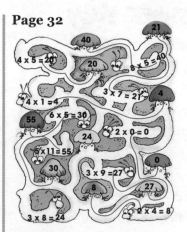

Page 33

A. 36   B. 50   D. 16   E. 44   G. 12
H. 18   I. 28   L. 30   M. 32   N. 27
O. 21   P. 0   R. 22   S. 35   T. 45
U. 24   W. 25   Y. 48   !. 9;
SO THAT HIS GROUP WOULD
BEGIN TO GET LARGER AND
MULTIPLY!;
Mr Weaver's class has 24 students.
Mrs Moore's class has 20 students.
Mr Weaver's class has more students.

Page 34

A. 22   B. 7   C. 18   D. 48   E. 36
G. 16   H. 60   I. 12   M. 44   O. 21
P. 40   R. 30   S. 45   T. 35   U. 28
V. 33   Y. 24   !. 0;
BECAUSE YOU HAVE THE
RIGHT PRODUCT EVERY TIME!;
36 crackers

Page 35

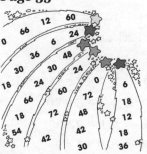

48 fireworks.

Page 36

1. 3 × 6 = 18   2. 6 × 5 = 30
3. 9 × 6 = 54   4. 11 × 6 = 66
5. 6 × 2 = 12   6. 4 × 6 = 24

7. $8 \times 6 = 48$ 8. $7 \times 6 = 42$
9. $6 \times 12 = 72$ 10. $0 \times 6 = 0$
11. $1 \times 6 = 6$ 12. $10 \times 6 = 60$
13. 30, ★ × ✓ = ☺〰
14. 42, ✓ × ⅄ = ⇦☒
15. 54, ✓ × ◆ = ★⇦
16. 18, ✓ × ☺ = ●↙
17. 48, ✓ × ↙ = ⇦↙
18. 36, ✓ × ✓ = ☺✓
19. 72, ⌘ × ✓ = ⅄☒
20. 60, ✓ × ☺ = ✓〰;
72 flower symbols

Page 37
Multiply by 5: 0, 5, 10, 15, 20, 25, 30, 35, 40, 45, 50, 55, 60;   Multiply by 6: 0, 6, 12, 18, 24, 30, 36, 42, 48, 54, 60, 66, 72

Page 38
1. 60   2. 15   3. 14   4. 10   5. 24   6. 12
7. 45   8. 40   9. 9   10. 0   11. 27   12. 25

Page 39
1. 8   2. 18   3. 50   4. 42   5. 28   6. 0
7. 32   8. 6   9. 16   10. 15   11. 40   12. 24

Page 40

42 months; no

Page 41

49 times

Page 42

Page 43
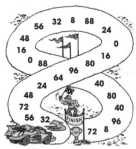
96 seconds

Page 44
1. 16, 32, 32, 80   2. 0, 40, 48, 72
3. 8, 24, 16, 88   4. 8, 96, 24, 48
5. 40, 64, 0   6. 72, 56, 64

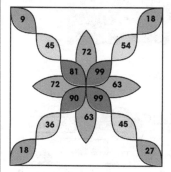

Page 45
Multiply by 7: 0, 7, 14, 21, 28, 35, 42, 49, 56, 63, 70, 77, 84
Multiply by 8: 0, 8, 16, 24, 32, 40, 48, 56, 64, 72, 80, 88, 96

Page 46
1. one hundred eight, $12 \times 9 = 108$
2. ninety-nine, $11 \times 9 = 99$
3. ninety, $10 \times 9 = 90$
4. eighty-one, $9 \times 9 = 81$
5. seventy-two, $8 \times 9 = 72$
6. sixty-three, $7 \times 9 = 63$

7. fifty-four, $6 \times 9 = 54$
8. forty-five, $5 \times 9 = 45$
9. thirty-six, $4 \times 9 = 36$;
The other factor in the multiplication sentence is one less each time; $3 \times 9 = 27$; $2 \times 9 = 18$; $1 \times 9 = 9$; $0 \times 9 = 0$

Page 47
Across	Down
1. Forty-five	2. Twenty-seven
5. Nine	3. Fifty-four
7. One hundred eight	4. Zero
10. Ninety	6. Seventy-two
11. Ninety-nine	9. Eighty-one

Page 48
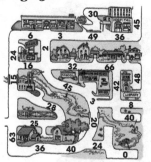

Page 49
A. 6   C. 45   D. 56   E. 25   F. 24
G. 16   H. 64   I. 90   K. 36   L. 84
M. 72   N. 49   O. 12   P. 18   R. 60
S. 27   T. 96   U. 81   Y. 108   !. 0;
FIND THE RIGHT PRODUCTS, GET THEM TO STICK IN YOUR HEAD AND DON'T LET THEM ESCAPE!

Page 50
The sum is 108. 12×9 or 9×12

Page 51

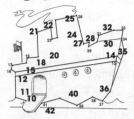

42 bananas, 20 coconuts

Page 52

48	36	72	96
63	49	27	99
49	24	56	7
64	45	35	80
54	81	21	36
77	40	18	63
9	45	35	27
70	42	72	72

28 tiles

Page 53

Page 54

Page 55

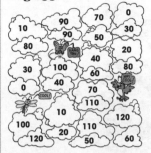

70 clouds

Page 56

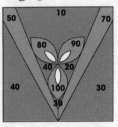

Page 57

Multiply 9: 0, 9, 18, 27, 36, 45, 54, 63, 72, 81, 90, 99, 108

Multiply 10: 0, 10, 20, 30, 40, 50, 60, 70, 80, 90, 100, 110, 120

Page 58

1. 10   2. 24   3. 64   4. 70   5. 45   6. 14
7. 81   8. 30   9. 24   10. 0   11. 28   12. 18

Page 59

1. 32   2. 80   3. 40   4. 21   5. 0   6. 12
7. 20   8. 0   9. 49   10. 27   11. 18   12. 40

Page 60

Page 61

		^{1}2	^{2}1		^{3}1	^{4}2
^{5}1		^{6}6	^{7}4		^{8}0	
^{9}8	^{10}1		^{11}4	^{12}5		
	^{13}4	^{14}2		^{15}6	^{16}3	
^{17}3		^{18}5	^{19}5		^{20}6	
^{21}2	^{22}4		^{23}4	^{24}0		

Page 62

1. 5   2. 8   3. 11   4. 0   5. 6
6. 10   7. 12   8. 16   9. 18   10. 24;
"TIME TO TAKE OFF."

Page 63

1. 2, 4, 6, 8   2. 4, 8, 12, 16
3. 6, 12, 18, 24   4. 8, 16, 24, 32
5. 10, 20, 30, 40, 50, 60, 70, 80,
   90, 100

Page 64

2 inches; 4 inches; Two possible answers: 6 inches, because it grew 2 inches each week; or 8 inches, because it doubled in height each week

Page 65

1. (people)(people)(people), 3 × 3 = 9
2. (people)(people)(people), 5 × 3 = 15
3. (people)(people), 8 × 2 = 16

Page 66

1. $5 × 4 = $20
2. $1 × 4 = $4
3. $2 × 10 = $20

Page 67

1. 12 × 3 = 36 toys
2. 12 × 5 = 60 loaves
3. 3 × 8 = 24 DVDs

Pages 68–74

1. B   2. A   3. C   4. D   5. B
6. B   7. A   8. D   9. D   10. D
11. C   12. C   13. C   14. B   15. C
16. D   17. B   18. C   19. A   20. A
21. 3 × 4 = 12   22. 5 × 3 = 15
23. 4 × 5 = 20
24. 3 km × 12 = 36 km
25. $7 × 10 = $70
26. 5 × 8 = 40 tickets

Learning Express

Congratulations!

I, _____

am a Scholastic Superstar!

I have completed Multiplication L2.

Paste a photo or draw a
picture of yourself.

Presented on _____

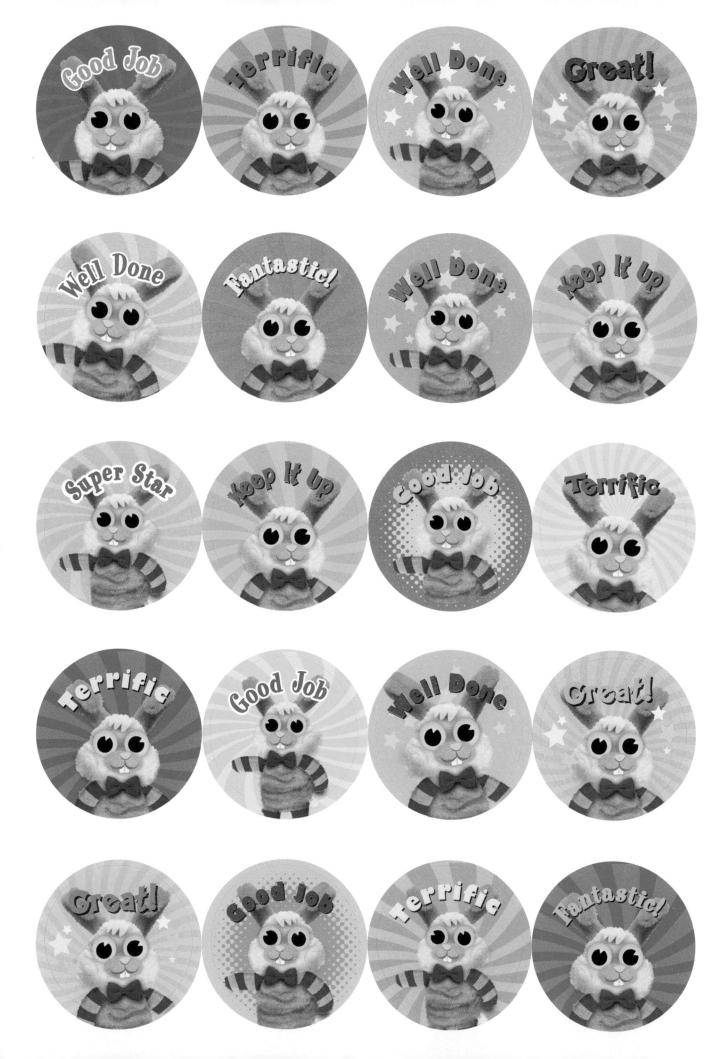